*"In the Koran, the first thing God said
to Muhammad was 'Read.' "*
—Alia Muhammad Baker

From the *New York Times*, July 27, 2003

The Librarian of Basra

A True Story from Iraq

WRITTEN & ILLUSTRATED BY

JEANETTE WINTER

HARCOURT, INC. Orlando Austin New York San Diego Toronto London

PRINTED IN SINGAPORE

Alia Muhammad Baker is the librarian of Basra,
a port city in the sand-swept country of Iraq.

Her library is a meeting place for all who love books.
They discuss matters of the world
and matters of the spirit.

Until now—now, they talk only of war.

Alia worries that the fires of war will destroy the books,
which are more precious to her than mountains of gold.
The books are in every language—new books, ancient books,
even a biography of Muhammad that is seven hundred years old.
She asks the governor for permission
to move them to a safe place.
He refuses.

So Alia takes matters into her own hands.
Secretly, she brings books home every night,
filling her car late after work.

The whispers of war grow louder.
Government offices are moved into the library.
Soldiers with guns wait on the roof.
Alia waits—and fears the worst.

Then . . . rumors become reality.

War reaches Basra.

The city is lit with a firestorm of bombs and gunfire.

Alia watches as library workers, government workers,
and soldiers abandon the library.
Only Alia is left to protect the books.

She calls over the library wall to her friend Anis Muhammad,
who owns a restaurant on the other side. "Can you help me
save the books?"

"I can use these curtains to wrap them."

"Here are crates from my shop."

"Can you use these sacks?"

"The books must be saved."

All through the night, Alia, Anis, his brothers,
and shopkeepers and neighbors take the books
from the library shelves, pass them over the seven-foot wall,
and hide them in Anis's restaurant.

The books stay hidden as the war rages on.

Then, nine days later, a fire burns the library to the ground.

The next day, soldiers come to Anis's restaurant.

"Why do you have a gun?" they ask.

"To protect my business," Anis replies.

The soldiers leave without searching inside.

They do not know that the whole of the library

is in my restaurant, thinks Anis.

At last, the beast of war moves on.
Alia knows that if the books are to be safe,
they must be moved again,
while the city is quiet.
So she hires a truck to bring all thirty thousand books
to her house and to the houses of friends.

In Alia's house, books are everywhere,
filling floors and cupboards and windows—

leaving barely enough room for anything else.

Alia waits.

She waits for war to end.

She waits, and dreams of peace.

She waits . . .

and dreams of a new library.

But until then, the books are safe—
safe with the librarian of Basra.

A Note from the Author

The invasion of Iraq reached Basra on April 6, 2003. With the help of friends and neighbors, Alia Muhammad Baker, chief librarian of Basra's Central Library, managed to rescue seventy percent of the library's collection before the library burned nine days later.

These events were first revealed to the world by *New York Times* reporter Shaila K. Dewan, who heard about Alia and the library during a visit to Anis Muhammad's restaurant, the Hamdan—which is near the library and is known as one of the best in Basra. Shaila's translator said Anis had an incredible story to tell about the war, so Shaila made an appointment to talk with him. Alia joined the discussion, and together they went on to share this amazing story.

Soon after the library was destroyed, Alia suffered a stroke and had heart surgery. But she is healing, and despite all, she is determined to see that the library is rebuilt.

For Allyn Johnston

Many thanks to Shaila K. Dewan, who uncovered the story of Alia Muhammad Baker and reported it in the *New York Times* on July 27, 2003.

www.HarcourtBooks.com

Library of Congress Cataloging-in-Publication Data
Winter, Jeanette.
The librarian of Basra: a true story from Iraq/Jeanette Winter.
p. cm.
1. Baker, Alia Muhammad—Juvenile literature. 2. Librarians—Iraq—Basrah—Biography—Juvenile literature.
3. Libraries—Destruction and pillage—Iraq—Basrah—Juvenile literature. 4. Iraq War, 2003—Juvenile literature. I. Title.
Z720.B24W56 2005
020'.92—dc22 2004012969
ISBN 0-15-205445-6

First edition
A C E G H F D B

The illustrations in this book were done in acrylic and pen on Arches watercolor paper.
The display lettering was created by Judythe Sieck.
The text type was set in Futura Medium.
Color separations by Bright Arts Ltd., Hong Kong
Printed and bound by Tien Wah Press, Singapore
This book was printed on totally chlorine-free Stora Enso Matte paper.
Production supervision by Ginger Boyer
Designed by Judythe Sieck